Anxious to Awesome

A handheld, unique change in perspective on child anxiety
With change comes transformation

Satsie Thomas
Art by Matthew King

Anxious to Awesome

**A handheld, unique change in perspective on child anxiety
With change comes transformation**

By **Satsie Thomas**
Art by **Matthew King** | matthew@mindpipe.co.uk

©2022 GillyBean Publishing All rights reserved.
No part of this publication may be reproduced, stored in a retrieval system or transmitted in any form or by any means, electronic, mechanical, photocopying, recording or otherwise without the prior permission of the publisher or in accordance with the provisions of the Copyright, Designs and Patents Act 1988 or under the terms of any licence permitting limited copying issued by the Copyright Licencing Agency.

Every effort has been made to ensure the information within the books is accurate at the date of publishing. The author and publisher do not hold any responsibility for misinterpretation, errors and/or omissions. Our books are solely for motivational and informational purposes only.

ISBN: **9798370402999**
Imprint: **Independently published**

satsiethomas.com

If your child is feeling overwhelmingly scared or worried and this is affecting their behaviour, reading this book will give you comfort and the ability to support your child to feel better and empowered.

You can begin this by knowing they were not born anxious, they were born to be creative; to invent, be entrepreneurial and build and to inspire others with their imaginative personalities. What has happened is something in the past has transpired to make them feel worried for a long while and when this fusion of personality type combines with a troubled environment, an anxiety disorder is the result. Simply put, it means they have adrenaline overload.

This is now the time to encourage your child to feel strong and embrace who they are. Remind them that they are capable and, through your normalizing behaviour, bring about change.

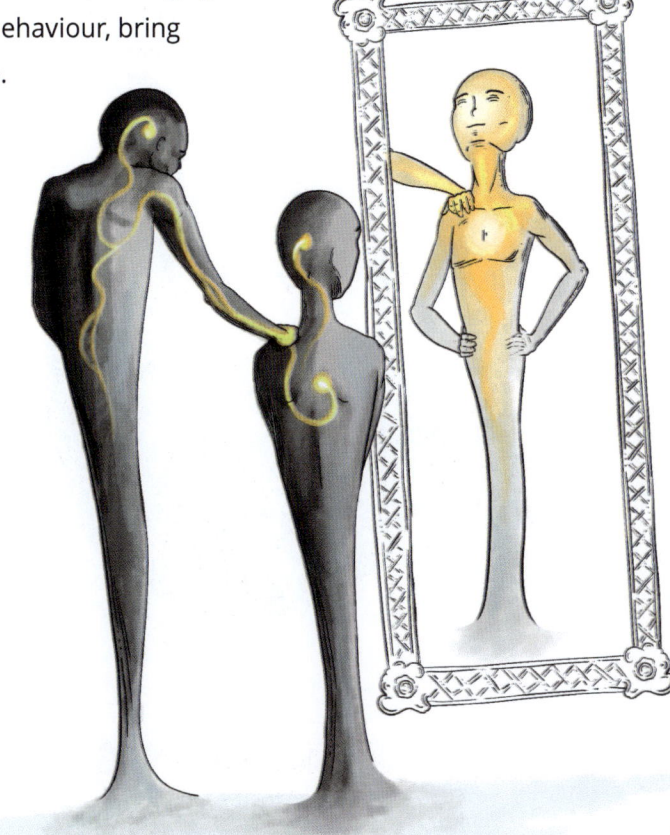

It's important for you to remember that *things have happened* in their life. Things that were not always good. Children do not have big backstories, so the catalysts are fairly easy to detect. You can help them to look back at past events over which they had no control and acknowledge that, through their environment, there has been a change in their physiology (*not* psychology).

It's important to reinforce the idea that *if those things (catalysts) had not occurred, then they would feel normal now*. It is the *effect* of what happened that has resulted in months, maybe even years, of worry, resulting in adrenaline levels which have reset too high.

The anxiety disorder, in many cases, comes long after the catalyst.

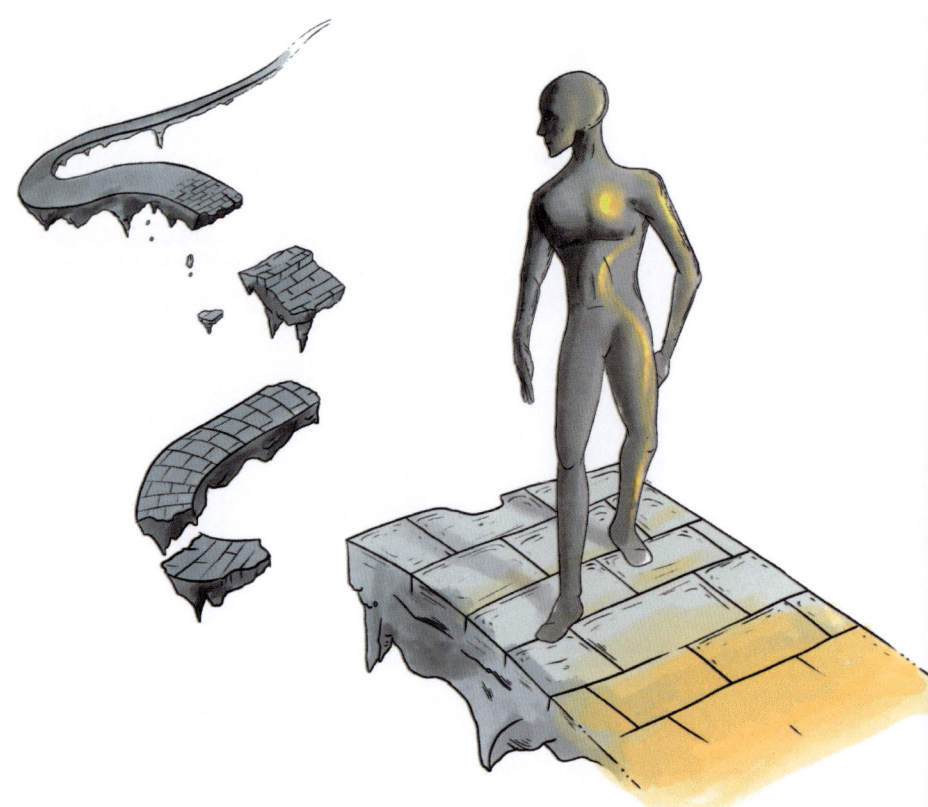

When a child is frightened, or overly worrying, they may experience extreme feelings of foreboding and dread, feel sick or be sensitive to loud noises and light. They may develop bowel issues.

Make them realise this is normal and natural and that even though it feels unpleasant, it's nothing to worry about. They've already recognised the causes of their feelings, so reinforce this recognition; that the feelings are a *result* of having been worried and anxious for so long, that worrying about anything is the same as being scared - it releases adrenaline and this affects almost all of the body.

The primary driver of stress and anxiety is adrenaline, the hormone which controls our fight-or-flight response. Tell them that everyone has this hormone and that it optimises survival if they are being attacked physically by temporarily increasing alertness ('what if' thoughts) reactions and even their strength! But too much adrenaline over a long period of time can have a very negative effect, leading to long term anxiety conditions like IBS, staying indoors and a host of other behaviours linked with how they feel inside.

The hormone adrenaline is part of human evolution, and was vital to the survival of our ancestors, but was only triggered in short bursts. In the modern day world it can be triggered constantly. This is when the body will alter and reset, leaving children with GAD (Generalised Anxiety Disorders).

So, long after the event, your child has feelings of fear caused by their body resetting their level of adrenaline. This permanent state of fear feeds yet *more* fear and is exacerbated if the grown-ups seem worried too.

Does your child feel shaky, panicky, and edgy all the time? Have they gone off food, have a sore stomach or react to loud noises? Have they stopped wanting to go to school? For them to answer these questions, they need to understand the reasons behind the feelings. Present them with this analogy (which is also found in their own book):

Imagine if, every morning, they wake up and exercise their arms. Over time the muscles will grow. But, instead of their arms, they exercise their adrenaline, by worrying and feeling scared. Like their muscles, their adrenaline will grow and reset to a new 'normal' high.

They've grown it so much it leaves them feeling nervous all the time. When they feel like this, it can make them want to shut themselves away, and anxiety loves boredom, so it only gets worse.

This is especially true of boys, as puberty will often be inhibited, even growth stunted. At a time when they should feel strong and masculine, they can be left feeling weak and shaky.

You might worry that this has happened out of the blue. However, it isn't something that's suddenly popped into existence, it's an outward manifestation of the long-term inner turmoil.

Reacting hastily, perhaps with a visit to the doctor for tests, or showing your child how worried you are about them, will have a negative effect. Your child will pick up on your emotions and it may make them *more* scared. Remember that it is the past experiences which cause the emotions (adrenaline) to be triggered over a period of time that has reset. Empower them to think differently by your behaviour being calm and relaxed.

Anxiety is a feeling, and feelings are held in the body. This means anxiety is not a mental health issue, but a *physiological* one. By reacting to anxiety as physiological and not psychological, your simple changes will help your child enormously.

This book is not directed at the habits, whether good or bad, that are formed from the anxiety and the way your child feels. It aims to give you a base level understanding to reverse and prevent the condition worsening. It 'shifts the behaviour' and tells your child to not add worry onto worry. Repeated worry and anxiety will reset your child's adrenaline at another higher level.

This book is designed to help alter your perspective, to enable you to help your child answer these questions: **How do I make my adrenaline go down? How do I get back to feeling normal?** It is to help you realise they do not have a mental health issue and, through understanding and then new behaviour, aid you in supporting their recovery.

There was a catalyst which caused your child's adrenaline levels to rise, but it is not permenant and can be reversed.

By reading their own book, your child is realising that they are *normal*! Not 'strange' or different from any of their peers. They should have acknowledged they have lived, witnessed or felt worried and that this has resulted in their G.A.D.

Help them to recognise those past events; to see they are not weak because of them but capable and brave; that they deserve to feel great again and that they're worthy.

Once they have recognised these things we can get to work!

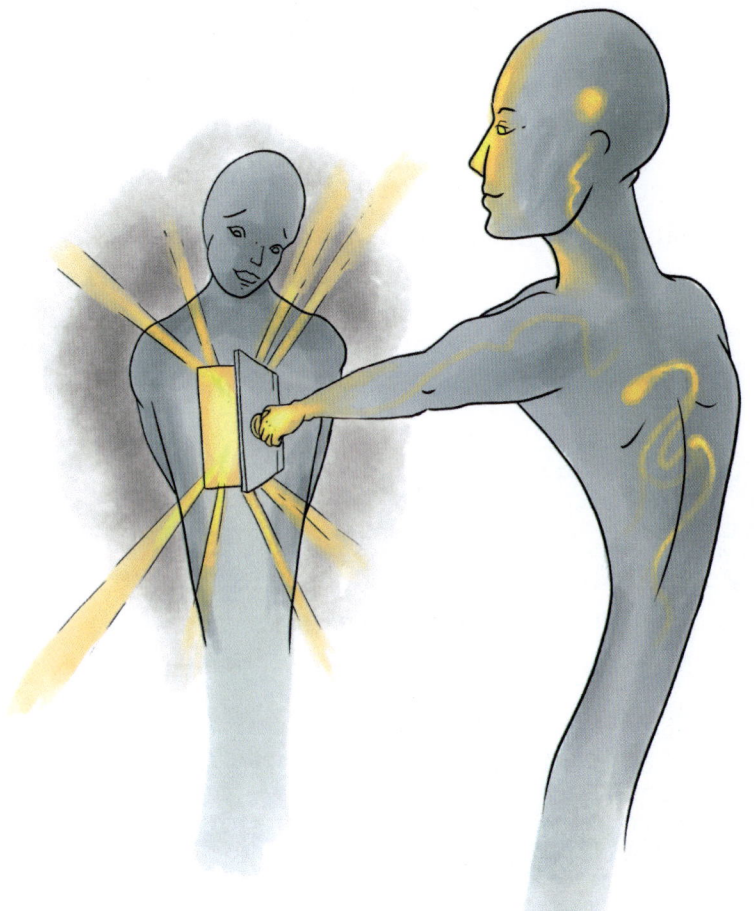

First, you must know this. It is **adrenaline** that is making them feel shaky and nervous. By falling into a cycle of rumination and overly worrying, your child has increased their level of adrenaline. But it is possible to reverse this. By behaving calmly and from this book no longer worrying it is a mental condition, you can help your child achieve this reduction, and lead them back to feeling like themselves once more.

By not engaging in the drama and being normal you will not believe the difference! What they need to support their recovery is a strength that they *can only get from you*.

In your child's book we ask them to imagine their sensations are a pan filled with cold milk from the fridge. It's chilled. We ask them to imagine it beginning to bubble as they put it on the hob and turn up the heat. If they turn up the heat too much the pan will boil over, the same way a panic attack feels like all their emotions are boiling over.

By behaving calmly and normally, treating them firmly but kindly (because you know this is not mental and their body is normal, it has simply reset the adrenaline levels to a simmer) your child will pick up on your new dynamic and this will set the scene for them to feel more confident.

They will try to project their aggression on to *you* (a textbook adrenaline symptom). They will try to create drama to match their inner turmoil. Don't feed into this, shut it down and be firm by removing yourself from the situation.

Your child's sensations are perfectly normal. Adrenaline is integral to our fight or flight response, but your child's worry has caused a failure of this response to 'switch off'. They may feel confusion with the knowledge that there is no danger yet they feel as though there *is*.

This can lead to them into thinking there is something 'wrong' with them but you can help them to acknowledge that there isn't. They are not in danger, and they don't need to hide away or feel scared, but they *do* feel real sensations of fear.
It's vital to recognise that is all they are: *sensations*.

By acknowledging this it is possible to 'reset' your child's internal physiology.

It's imperative that your child allows themselves to experience their sensations now with knowledge and understanding and not with fear, despite the discomfort. It is essential that they know the sensations are harmless.

In their book we ask them to imagine they go and see a scary film with their friends. It makes them scared, jumpy and frightened. But when they leave the cinema, they naturally switch off the fear response as they think about something else (like going for food perhaps) and, without even realising, their subconscious will shut off the fear response. They can enjoy the rest of the evening calmly, simply because the logical front brain told their back brain it was just a film and then diverted the thoughts to something else.

This diversion of thought needs to happen every day until the body has readjusted and settled back to normal. It can only be done when *you* and your child use your knowledge and power to switch it off, like at the cinema.

This same principle applies with G.A D (always having adrenaline in your system) If they begin to feel anxious, confidently remind them - It is just adrenaline and feels awful but will not hurt you. They have the capability to reverse the adrenaline by going about their business as though nothing were wrong. They are telling their adrenaline, **"Everything is OKAY, you can go away now!"**

Please know some of the past causes can be one, or even all, of these:

- *Bereavement fear*
- *Bullying scares*
- *Pre-Divorce and Post-Divorce worries*
- *Sickness and Illness scares (for themselves or loved ones)*

If your child is experiencing nightmares or having trouble getting to sleep, you can reassure them (and yourself) by having them see it is the raised adrenaline causing the issue. They are on 'high alert' even while they sleep, with their mind distorting anxious thoughts from their day.

Speak normally to them in a matter-of-fact tone. Explain that you and they know this is just their adrenaline, and then confidently walk out. This shows them you are not worried. Your behaviour will give them confidence to do this themselves.

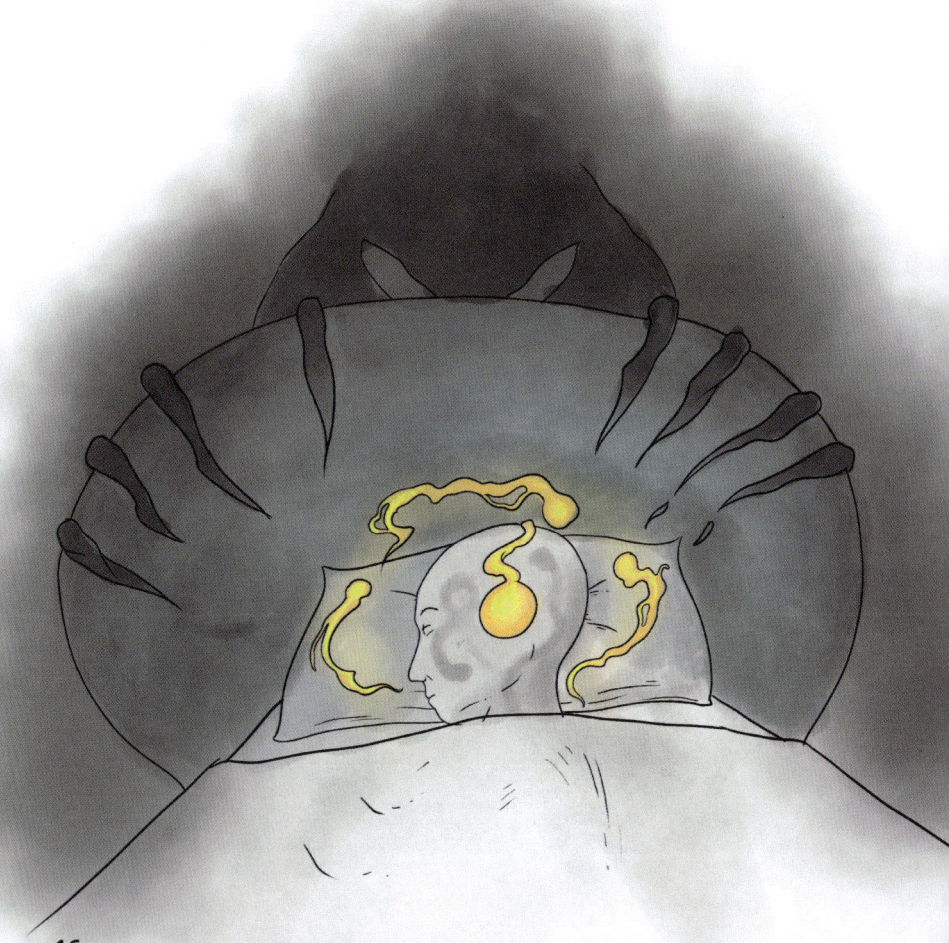

This year can be a catalyst for change! Why not encourage your child to start trying to do some of the things that usually cause them anxiety. They might worry they'll embarrass themselves or have a panic attack, *but they won't*. If they allow themselves to try, they will realise how strong they can be. Encourage them to think about how they wish their life could be, about how to be happy again. Give them the support to make it happen.

And remember this is your life too! You want to be happy, not worried, so make this happen for the whole family.

Encourage them to use the book as a distraction tool when feeling overwhelmed.

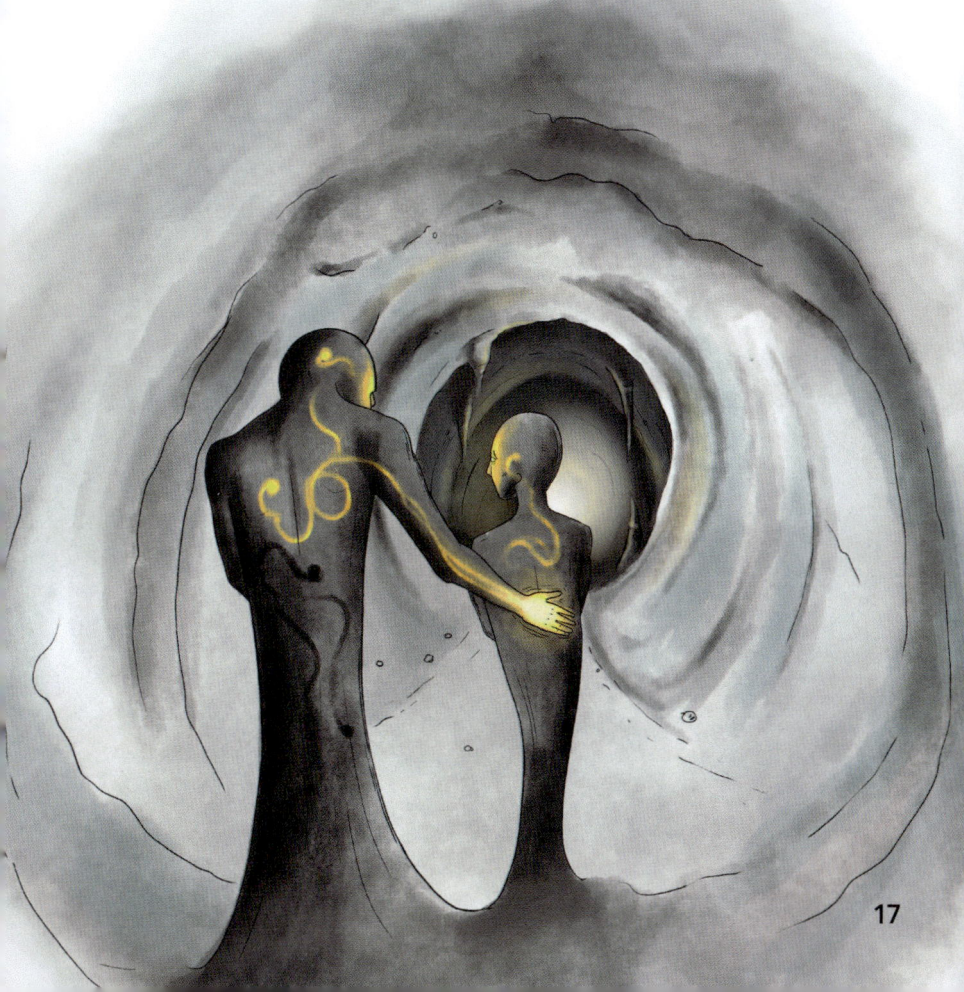

Do you know what a panic attack actually is?

When you eat too much, your body jumps into autopilot and makes you sick. At the time it feels awful but, ultimately, it's harmless and perfectly natural. Well, a panic attack is the same, only it's caused by a surplus of adrenaline. The body jumps into autopilot and 'ejects' the adrenaline in the form of a panic attack. Just like being sick, it might feel horrible, but it's harmless.

It is even possible to 'trick' the body into avoiding the attack in the first place. By acknowledging the possibility of the attack and allowing it, it will most likely not take place. Usually, it is the fear of a panic attack that brings one on.

So if your child is becoming overwhelmed (boiling over) distract them, or have them say **"GO ON THEN! Bring it on!"** This will almost certainly stop it in its tracks. It sounds odd, but try it !

All our books are about making knowledge your power and recognising that counterintuitive behaviours can be effective.

As the saying goes...
**If you do what you've always done,
you will get what you've always got.**

Hopefully by now your child knows *why* they began to feel anxious and afraid. Also, you are realising that, despite your instincts naturally causing you to worry, there are techniques that both you and your child can employ to overcome their negative emotions.

It is important that they recognise the role of adrenaline and that they must never let a hormone stop them doing anything they want to do!

**The more they come to realise this,
the more confident they'll feel.**

So, make this year the best you've had for ages! Your child should have gleaned some valuable insights from their book, so capitalise on that by asking them what they'd like to do, where they'd like to go!

And then make it happen.

By not letting their adrenaline overwhelm them, by their new understanding that anxiety is not mental (it is *physiological*), they can apply this to the challenges—they can 'reset' and, in time, reduce their base-level adrenaline back to normal.

To better support your child on this journey, keep in mind these counter-intuitive tips:

If they feel panic, You can say well *"lets get on with it, it won't hurt and after you will feel great"* Try it, it feels crazy but it works!

Though this may sound counter-intuitive too, talking about past traumas makes it worse. Knowing they are what *began* the anxiety is enough, you do not need to bring it all up again.

Support your child, but don't let them rely wholly on you. Remind them they are strong and have the power within themselves to do this.

And if your child becomes angry, try to respond calmly without becoming angry yourself. It might be hard, but adrenaline loves anger, don't get involved in the drama.

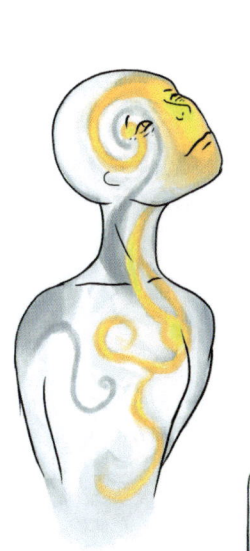
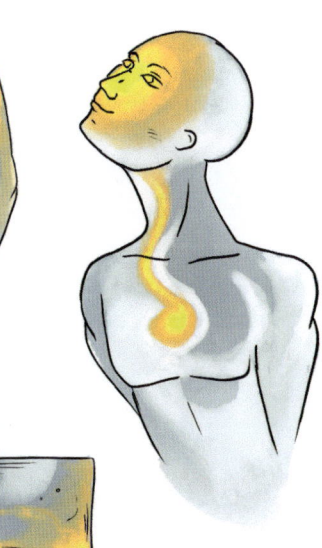

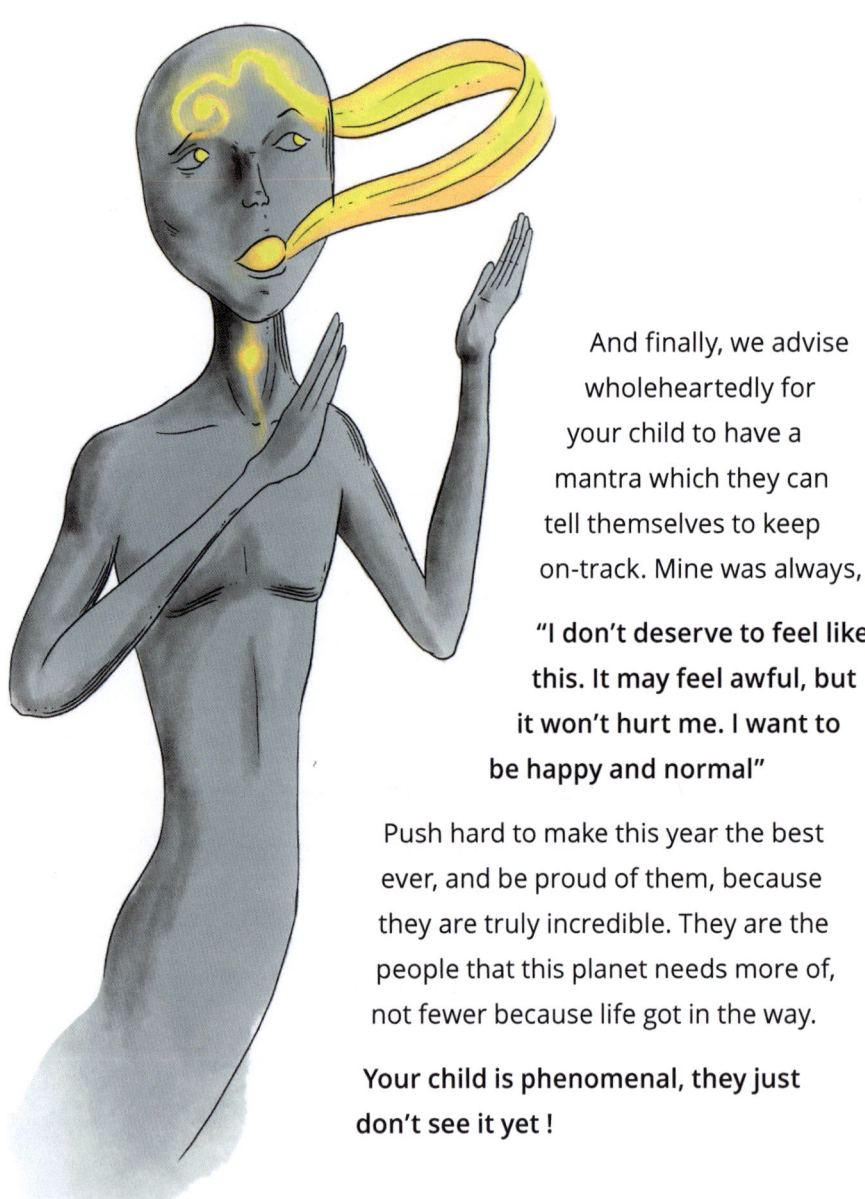

And finally, we advise wholeheartedly for your child to have a mantra which they can tell themselves to keep on-track. Mine was always,

"I don't deserve to feel like this. It may feel awful, but it won't hurt me. I want to be happy and normal"

Push hard to make this year the best ever, and be proud of them, because they are truly incredible. They are the people that this planet needs more of, not fewer because life got in the way.

Your child is phenomenal, they just don't see it yet !

The *Bug to Butterfly* Series

- **School Refusal** (Free Teachers Guide)
- **Eliminate the Panic Attack**
- **Knowing how to stop Self-Harming**
- **Understanding ADHD is Anxiety**
- **Get to know Anxiety & Gender Change**
- **Seeing Anorexia in a new light**
- **Anxious sensitivities from light & Sound**
- **Explaining Emetophobia** (fear of sickness)
- **Child/Parent guide to eliminating Derealisation**
- **Why such Rapid Aggression and Irritability?**
- **Anxiety and Migraines**
- **Panic and Fainting Uncovered**
- **Hallucinations & Voices – The unscary revelation**
- **Why OCD is Anxiety**
- **Deep Dive into the weird and upsetting visions**
- **How Rituals can be stopped in days**
- **Reversing the skin conditions** (Styes, Boils)
- **Reversing the phobias**
- **Getting to go back to sleep after Nightmares/Night Frights**

Printed in Great Britain
by Amazon